TO SAIL NO MORE

PART TWO

Mike Critchley

INTRODUCTION

The First Part of this somewhat sad book was so well received that we have been encouraged - indeed badgered -into producing a second - and even third part.

I am sure any ex -naval readers will agree with me that, as they flick through the photographs reproduced here it can be quite a shock to see amongst them pictures that instantly provoke the response of "That's my old ship....is that what they did to her"

For me, to see pictures of ARK ROYAL being eased off to the scrapyard were just so different from my first sight - and lingering mental picture of that carrier as I joined by boat - at sunrise - whilst she lay at anchor in Mombasa Harbour. A fine sight indeed as the sun rose that day in '66 and so different to the lifeless hulk shown within these pages....... The photos of the once mighty battleship VANGUARD brought back distant memories, so easily, of gazing into her mighty boilers on a "Field trip" with the school CCF....... The picture of the battered frigate VENUS could only remind me of my first trip to sea - again as a member of the CCF as she took our group from Plymouth to Fowey during one annual camp. We thought, incidentally, we had gone half way round the world - at the tender age of 13..... Like many others TENBY was my "home" for three months as a Cadet as part of our training at Dartmouth College. Will I ever forget painting that same mast, as seen here, in the pouring rain in Portland Harbour one Sunday morning.... ("Good for the Soul" they said at the time!) .... Oh yes, I well remember being bounced overnight to navigate the KEPPEL - and no one even said a brief "thank you" ...... and as for my time in her sister BLACKWOOD I have mixed memories of some great people I served alongside - and equally great seas off Iceland. The latter putting enormous strains on both ship - and stomach!

Just a picture of BULWARK will have many a matelots memory flooding back to the prolonged withdrawal from Malta in the early seventies; to say nothing of the experience of missing her on sailing - twice - within three weeks........ or the horrific boiler room fire off Italy. MINERVA .... wasn't that the ship Prince Charles was serving in when I flew ahead of them all to escape the North Atlantic gales and organise the press - and then for both of us to escape with our lives when a crazed gunman broke into the Governor's residence in Bermuda killing the Governor, his ADC and dog, but missing his real target by 24 hours.......

FORTH..... would anyone ever forget that huge lump of steel stopping for a Wardroom Mess dinner in the midst of the South China Sea and we guests from the escorting destroyer being invited to climb a very frail rope ladder up that huge ship's side - to claim our meal. It seemed far easier leaving for some reason..........LION home for my Midshipman's fleet board whilst in Malta.......TROUBRIDGE - why did no one ever say a simple thanks for extinguishing what could have become a major fire onboard whilst the whole crew were ashore in refit.....and that picture of GALATEA was that really the immaculately presented RN contribution to the German Kiel week I remember so well....

I could go on...... as I'm told us old sailors do ..... but I trust many readers will too when they see snaps of their old steamers that can only bring back a memory . Hopefully many of them will be as good as mine but I must admit I included the picture of the last remains of DAINTY on page 1 for no other reason than a ship that seemed to give so many of her ship's company so many bad memories of her last commission that it was a real joy to see her being ripped apart at the end of her career!

I trust you can evoke some happy memories as you read this our latest offering - and if you find a few similar photos - of good quality - please send them in for us to look at as we start work on Part 3

Mike Critchley   Liskeard   November 1998

All good things come to an end. Many readers will have experienced paying off a warship which was their "home" for a number of years. Within a very few days Paying Off ceremonies have been held... stores and fuel landed, men left for new ships and establishments. Soon a living ship is just a hulk and a memory - simply no longer required for further service. Here HMS FALMOUTH leaves the port of Falmouth for the last time in 1984. In this instance it was a second "final farewell". FALMOUTH had paid off in 1982 into the Standby Squadron and was not expected to go to sea again but the Falklands crisis changed all that...........

(RN Photo)

For ten years after World War II many ports around the UK were host to a wide variety of warships. Such was the requirement to lay ships up that many non dockyard ports were pressed into service but here at Portsmouth this photograph (taken in 1955) shows (from right to left) the cruisers LIVERPOOL and MAURITIUS, the destroyer DAINTY and frigate VERULAM. In the centre (right) are seen the frigates RAPID, TUSCAN, and LOCH TRALAIG. Astern of them are the minesweepers WATERWITCH (nearest), ACUTE and JEWEL. At the front of the photograph can be seen three destroyers FINISTERRE (front), with CAPRICE and TRAFALGAR to the rear. A visitor to this area today would hardly recognise this part of Portsmouth Harbour with the cross channel ferry port and motorway system dominating.

(RN Photo)

LAID UP - PORTSMOUTH

Another photograph from the upper reaches of Portsmouth Harbour. Here HMS VOLAGE (left) is probably alongside the frigates ORWELL and RAPID but as the photograph is undated it cannot be confirmed.

(R N Photo)

Affectionately known throughout the fleet as "the old grey ghost of the Borneo coast" as a result of her long service in the Far East during confrontation, the Commando carrier HMS ALBION is seen here at the end of her days as a Royal Navy warship. Photographed in April 1973 plans were afoot for a further (mercantile) use for her but despite being sold in October that year for conversion to a crane ship for service with the North Sea oil industry and being towed to the Clyde from Portsmouth for conversion for further service - nothing materialised. She was towed to Faslane on 16 November that year to be broken up.

(D Swetnam)

6

At the stroke of a pen a single Defence Review decided that the once numerically strong 'O' class of conventional submarine was no longer required. Efforts were made to sell these very successful submarines overseas but failed and consequently the submarines OTUS and OTTER are seen here laid up at Fareham Creek awaiting a buyer in the next MoD sale. With no fuel and no stores or weapons onboard these boats ride high in the quiet waters of the creek in December 1991. ENDURANCE, MINERVA & PHOEBE are seen in the trot to the rear.

(Maritime Photographic)

7

A full house after World War II. This photograph taken from the famous Brunel Railway Bridge across the Tamar shows a large number of frigates and destroyers laid up north of the bridge having been declared simply surplus to requirements. The pier in the foreground may still be seen, it services the Royal Naval armament depot at Ernesettle.

(S Goodman Collection)

LAID UP - PLYMOUTH

The monitor ROBERTS returned to Devonport from service in the Far East in November 1945 and was used as a turret drill ship, and then an accommodation ship for the Reserve Fleet at Devonport in 1963. She then spent almost two years in the River Tamar before being towed from Devonport on 19 July 1965. Some twenty years after entering the port.

(S Goodman Collection)

The battleship HOWE spent six years in reserve but the call for further service never did come. Here in this photograph taken in 1958 she spends her last few weeks laid up in the River Tamar before being towed off to Scotland for scrap.

(D Williams Collection)

The unmistakable lines of the carrier UNICORN seen here laid up at Devonport in 1955. After operational service during World War II she was placed in and out of reserve as a maintenance and replenishment carrier before service during the Korean War. Further roles included an emergency landing ship, a ferry carrier and eventually an aircraft supply and repair ship. She spent from 1955 in reserve until being towed to Troon in June 1959 for breaking up.

(D Williams Collection)

Another Korean War veteran. The light fleet aircraft carrier OCEAN spent the last four years of her life in reserve. She is seen here laid up in the Tamar before she too was towed to Scotland in May 1962 to be cut up.

(D Williams Collection)

Recognisable by a generation of naval officers as "their" training ships the frigates SCARBOROUGH and TENBY (rear) lie in the River Tamar. Having paid off in the autumn of 1972 and laid up at Devonport in March the following year SCARBOROUGH was towed from Devonport to the Tyne for survey but soon left again to return to Devonport. By 1974 a proposed sale to Pakistan had been cancelled and she returned to the Tyne. After some months laid up she was towed to Blyth where she was finally broken up. The proposed sale of TENBY to Pakistan was also cancelled and in June 1977 she was sold to Thomas Ward for breaking up in South Wales.

(S Goodman Collection)

After a career that saw her in service from the Cod War off Iceland to the Far East the frigate SALISBURY ended her days as the last RN diesel powered frigate afloat. In 1978 a proposed sale to Egypt was cancelled whilst on her delivery voyage to that country. By May 1980 she had arrived at Devonport after a spell laid up at Chatham and was used as a harbour training ship for HMS RALEIGH. Seen here in 1984 she had no further role for the RALEIGH trainees and was awaiting her fate which eventually turned out to be that of a target. She was sunk on 30th September 1985.

(Mike Critchley)

The mighty ARK. The aircraft carrier ARK ROYAL - flagship of many an Admiral, home for many more sailors and star of a very popular TV series - finalises her destoring which took most of 1979 in 5 Basin at Devonport Dockyard. All plans to preserve her had failed.

(S Goodman Collection)

Possibly the last photograph of the submarine NARWHAL. Seen here in August 1983 the submarine was towed from Devonport 24 hours later and sunk in a position some 15 miles south of Falmouth on 3 August. She had already been sunk and raised as an exercise during June 1980 (off Portland) and is now (1998) still available (on the sea bed) for the training of salvage personnel.

(Mike Critchley)

A strange sight on the River Tamar in October 1979. The submarine CACHALOT having paid off in September 1977 was expected to be sold to Egypt but this fell through and she was used - by donating her fin - to repair the submarine OLYMPUS after a collision . She remained at Devonport until February 1980 when she was towed away to Blyth for scrap.

(D G Thomas Collection)

The former coal exporting port of Penarth was used extensively to lay ships up. This shot, taken on 7 September 1954, shows mainly (unidentified) River and Castle Class vessels.

(Author's Collection)

LAID UP - SOUTH WALES

The Bute Docks at Cardiff - just a few miles from Penarth - were also extensively used to lay up ships after the War. Local residents will hardly be able to recognise this photograph after all the redevelopment in recent years.
(Welsh Industrial & Maritime Museum)

Full house at Llanelly North Dock. With commercial ports all around the coast being pressed into service to berth redundant warships after World War II. This aerial view of Llanelly North Dock shows how just one port did its bit taking all the excess tonnage of Landing Craft no longer required.

(Welsh Industrial & Maritime Museum)

A real reserve fleet warrior.... The corvette OXFORD CASTLE spent 1946-1949 in reserve at Devonport. A refit at Liverpool was undertaken in 1950 before she entered reserve at Devonport for two years. From 1952 to 1956 she lay idle in reserve at Penarth (as seen here) and was eventually placed on the disposal list in November 1956. She was offered to the Finnish Navy in 1957 but the deal did not materialise and in September 1960 she arrived at Briton Ferry to be broken up.

(D G Thomas Collection)

Penarth Dock during the summer of 1958. The destroyer in the foreground is HMS CASSANDRA which, unlike many other reserve fleet ships, was brought forward and went on to serve in the Mediterranean and Far East during the 60s. She eventually paid off in January 1966.

(Welsh Industrial & Maritime Museum)

The destroyer MATCHLESS was laid up at Penarth from 1952 to 1957 until sold in August of that year to Turkey. She was refitted at Govan before being handed over to Turkey in Glasgow in 1959. Her sister ship METEOR lies inboard, she spent the years 1953 to 1957 at Penarth before also being sold to Turkey.

(D G Thomas Collection)

23

The frigate ESKIMO ended her days in 1979 in the Standby Squadron at Chatham, but by 1980 was surplus to requirements and for disposal. However, as can be seen in this photograph (taken on 30 August 1990) she still had a role to fulfil. Seen here moored off Pembroke Dock she was used as a target by the Research Establishment at Aberporth. Outboard can just be seen the RMAS vessel DOLWEN - also for disposal.

24

(Richard Lindfield)

Once seen roaring around the Portland exercise areas the Fast Patrol Boat BRAVE BORDERER ended her days as a target on the Aberporth range too. She is seen here laid up at Pembroke Dock with various "weapon inflicted injuries" alongside an unknown Type 15 frigate.

(D G Thomas Collection)

Towed from Portsmouth on 14 December 1965 the submarine SEA SCOUT (right) and her sister SERAPH had an eventful voyage to the breakers. SEA SCOUT broke loose during the tow for 24 hours and had to be located by a naval helicopter before being brought into Swansea. The tides were not right for her to be towed up the River Neath so the interlude in Swansea - until 1 January 1966 - became necessary.

(N Denby)

26

Stories are still told in Portsmouth of the 4 August 1960 when the mighty battleship VANGUARD ran aground. The harbour was closed for most of the day as the tugs valiantly strove to get her back on her intended course for the scrapyard. The accident had occurred when a swing towards the Gosport side of the harbour earlier on during her final voyage out of harbour had been corrected - but by far too much! Your author, standing as a teenage schoolboy just yards away, thought it all a great day out but no doubt not an experience shared by the Admiralty pilots involved.

(D G Thomas Collection)

The cruiser GAMBIA ended her days as Flagship of the Flag Officer Flotillas - Home Fleet and paid off in 1960. She then spent many a year as part of the Reserve Fleet at Portsmouth. She is seen here in December 1968 starting out on her final voyage to the breakers at Inverkeithing.

(D G Thomas Collection)

Having been laid up in reserve in Portsmouth since 1961 the frigate ORWELL was eventually towed (June 1965) to the breakers in South Wales. The heavy cladding around the open bridge doubtless made it difficult for the pilot negotiating her out of harbour. She met up with her deep sea tug - the TYPHOON in the Solent and arrived in Newport (Wales) on 28 June.

(Mike Lennon)

Heading for Faslane the aircraft carrier VICTORIOUS leaves Portsmouth for the last time. It is generally agreed that her scrapping was a political decision - years before it was expected. A small fire onboard during a refit in 1967 was blamed for the decision to retire her early. She had undergone a massive reconstruction from 1950-1958 which had been expected to give her a further twenty years service life.

(Author's Collection)

20 November 1974 - the Battle class destroyer CORUNNA is eased from Portsmouth Harbour on her way to Sunderland to be broken up. As it turned out she remained at Sunderland for nearly a year before being towed to Blyth, in September 1975 for the work to commence. Note her lack of 965 radar aeriel at the top of her mast it was doubtless removed for service in another ship.
(Mike Lennon)

The camera never lies... The frigate BLACKPOOL, having returned from a period of loan service to the Royal New Zealand Navy, is towed from Portsmouth in March 1976 - heading for the Firth of Forth. Her usefulness to the Navy was not quite over as she was destined for service as a target ship. No doubt the extra masts were installed for monitoring equipment. She was eventually broken up at St David-on-Forth from May 1978 by J A White.

(Mike Lennon)

The tug DALMATIAN heads the frigate KEPPEL out of Portsmouth on 18 April 1979. Her days in the Fishery Protection, Londonderry and Portland Squadrons over. She was eventually broken up by Liguria Maritime Ltd at Sittingbourne.

(D Swetnam)

Memories of hectic days in mountainous seas off the Icelandic Coast during Fishery Protection duties fade as the empty hulk of the frigate BLACKWOOD is eased out of Portsmouth Harbour for her final voyage to the scrapyard. She is seen here on the 16 November 1976 heading for Troon.

(Mike Lennon)

Placed in reserve in 1976 the commando carrier BULWARK was brought back into service two years later and remained so until 1981. Despite tentative plans to reactivate her during the Falklands War these were not pursued (due to the cost) and she remained in Portsmouth Harbour until 10 April 1984 when tugs eased her past the active fleet on her way to Cairnryan in Scotland and the breakers. Many hundreds of ex sailors can tell you stories of their days on board the "Rusty B" as she was affectionately known.

(R N Photo)

Apart from a period in service in the Gulf from 1962 - 66 KEMERTON spent much of her career in reserve. Placed on the disposal list in May 1969 she was eventually sold, in October 1971, to Solent Power Units Ltd of Fareham. However, final demolition took place in Poole in 1975. Here "half a hulk" is towed from Portsmouth en-route to Poole.

(Mike Lennon)

Apart from the period in 1968-69 when she was in active service as the Far East Fleet maintenance ship BERRY HEAD spent much of her very long career in reserve. Having been built in 1944 in Canada she ended her days from 1976-87 as an accommodation and refit support ship at Devonport before being towed to the Reserve Fleet disposal trots at Portsmouth. It was February 1990 before she was eventually towed from Portsmouth for scrapping in Turkey.

(D Swetnam)

When photographs started appearing of redundant warships being sunk with their pennant numbers still showing, the Ministry of Defence, in respect to old sailors who were upset to see their former home disappear in such an ignominious fashion, decreed that pennant numbers would henceforth be painted out when vessels were heading for a watery grave. Here the frigate ARETHUSA leaves Portsmouth under tow on the 1st June 1991 for such a disposal. The emergency towing line rigged down the port side can clearly be seen.

(Walter Sartori)

The one that got away. As the O class submarines rapidly left their home at HMS DOLPHIN (Gosport) the submarine ONYX was saved by the Warship Preservation Trust as a memorial to all the submariners who went to the South Atlantic during the 1982 conflict. ONYX - the only diesel propelled submarine to take part in the Falklands War - is now (1998) on public display daily at Birkenhead.

(Walter Sartori)

No longer required by the RFA ... and with no navy interested in buying her for further service ... There was only one further voyage for the RFA tanker TIDESPRING to take. Seen here leaving Portsmouth on 20 March 1992 the tanker is heading for the scrapyards of India behind the huge Russian tug STAKHORVETS.

(Walter Sartori)

The frigate MINERVA - once the home for HRH The Prince of Wales - leaves Portsmouth on her final voyage. Sold to Indian breakers she was destined for an "interesting" journey on the long haul round the Cape of Good Hope to India. (See page 42)

(Walter Sartori)

The frigate CLEOPATRA was also towed out of harbour on 21 September 1993 with MINERVA as she too was destined for India. In order to save money the towage company attempted to tow both ships behind one tug. A move that doubtless cost them considerably more by the time the vessels arrived in India. They both broke loose from their tow in the Indian Ocean and drifted for a very long period before being taken into South Africa on their long haul to the breakers.

(Walter Sartori)

The ex RFA OLMEDA is seen here being eased out of Fareham Creek on 19 July 1994 for her final voyage. Her new owners registered her as the merchant ship NIAXCO so that she could steam with a skeleton crew for her final journey to the breakers - again in India.

(Walter Sartori)

An unusual one ... The former East German frigate ROSTOCK was destined to be sunk during a NATO exercise in the North Atlantic but as a result of pressure from environmental groups ended up in Portsmouth Harbour, rather than being sunk in the early 1990s. She remained in Portsmouth Harbour until 1998 when the decision was made to sell her and she eventually left, as seen here, on 14 July 1998 for Turkey behind the Russian tug SAPHIR thus closing a long, and sometimes embarrassing chapter, of the final years of her career.

(Walter Sartori)

Not easily recognised as a former warship but here what remains of the former HMS VULCAN (having been part of HMS DEFIANCE) is seen being towed past Drake's Island in December 1955 heading for the breakers.

(S Goodman Collection)

TOWED AWAY - PLYMOUTH

Launched in 1938 it was not until July 1985 that the submarine depot ship FORTH ended her days. Well known by generations of submariners throughout World War II and for many years after FORTH provided depot and maintenance facilities for hundreds of submarine crews from the Far East to the Mediterranean. From 1972 to 1978 she was renamed DEFIANCE when acting as Depot Ship for the Second Submarine Squadron at Devonport but by 1985 her time was up and she was towed from the River Tamar for her final voyage to the Medway to be broken up.

(S Goodman Collection)

Her days not quite over but the frigate MOHAWK is towed from Devonport on the 15th October 1979 to the Standby Squadron at Chatham after a short refit. However by August 1981 she was on the disposal list and a year later towed from the Medway to Cairnryan to be broken up. The outline of the carrier EAGLE can just be seen in the background.

(S Goodman Collection)

Most redundant warships slip out of Plymouth Harbour without anyone taking the slightest notice. However when something the size of the aircraft carrier EAGLE leaves port for the last time local residents - many doubtless having served onboard at some stage - turn out to shed a tear as she too departs for the breakers. She spent the last six years of her life laid up at Devonport simply to provide spares to keep her sister ship ARK ROYAL operational. By October 1978 that role too was complete and she was towed off to Cairnryan.

(S Goodman Collection)

The mighty ARK ROYAL leaves Devonport for the last time,with most of the port's tugs fussing round her to ease her through the narrows between Devon and Cornwall. The carrier heads for the open sea and Cairnryan. Don't be confused by the smoke coming from her funnel; a few "wags" in the towing crew had found a number of mattresses onboard which they set light to, to give the impression of her raising steam as she left harbour. Although many a tear was briefly shed by the public many who had sailed onboard her were not so emotive. Despite a major effort to preserve her many an ex-sailor will say that he was homesick onboard - she was their home and they were sick of it. Living accommodation for many was extremely poor during her final years of active service.

(S Goodman Collection)

The destroyer CAPRICE ended her seagoing days as a training ship for engineer officers based at Devonport but by March 1973 she had paid off for disposal. In October that year she was towed from Devonport for the Medway and the cutters' torches. The somewhat novel approach of towing her stern first from the port appears to be to save on harbour towing costs. Here ROBUST eases her through the harbour approaches and simply by letting go her berthing ropes could then take over as the deep sea tug to tow her through the English Channel - without the assistance of other harbour vessels.

(S Goodman Collection)

Aircraft carrier, officers' training ship and eventually a heavy repair ship the TRIUMPH fulfilled many a role during her service career. She however paid off into reserve at Chatham in 1972 and remained inactive until 1980 although kept in good condition for further service. By 1980 she was placed on the disposal list and eventually left Chatham on 9th December 1981 for Spain to be broken up. It was only a few months later, in April 1982, that the planners were desperate for a ship such as TRIUMPH which could have had a major role to fulfil as a repair/depot ship during the Falklands War. It was not to be - by then the cutters had already been at work and it was far too late to recover the situation.

(Mike Lennon)

The first nuclear submarine to pay off was DREADNOUGHT and she is seen here being towed from Chatham to Rosyth in 1984 whilst a decision was made on how to dispose of a "hot" nuclear powered submarine. She has remained in Rosyth ever since and today (1998) has been joined by a dozen other redundant nuclear submarines in UK Dockyard Ports. There is still no long term safe method of disposal of these vessels available in the UK.

(R N Photo)

An unnamed Bay Class frigate is towed down Channel by the tugs TRYPHON and ENVOY. This photograph gives a good view of the preservation methods employed around the weapon systems onboard.

(D G Thomas Collection)

53

With an extremely short service career behind her the cruiser LION was approved for scrapping in 1972 having only completed on the Tyne in 1960. She is seen here in the English Channel being towed to Rosyth where she arrived in May 1973 for reusable equipment to be stripped from her. It was a further two years before she arrived in Inverkeithing to be broken up.

(D G Thomas Collection)

Known to a generation of naval divers as their headquarters and deep diving ship the former salvage vessel RECLAIM eventually came to the end of her days and is seen here being towed up the English Channel to Belgium for scrap.

(Mike Lennon)

Having arrived off the South Wales coast with the frigate TROUBRIDGE the ocean going tug REWARD prepares to hand over the tow to a local tug for the final tow to Newport and the cutters torches.

(D J Lynch)

ARRIVING FOR SCRAP - SOUTH WALES

After many years service in Australia the submarine TRUMP ended her days in the smelters of the South Wales steel works. She is seen here arriving off the Newport deep having been towed to Wales by the tug SAMSONIA . The ocean going tug is seen here hauling her charge close in so that it can be handed over to the small local tugs for the final journey to the Cashmore Yard in Newport.

(D G Thomas)

The naval tug SAMSONIA was also responsible for towing TACITURN to the South Wales breakers of Thomas Ward. She is seen here arriving at Briton Ferry on the 8th August 1971.

(D G Thomas)

"Wales' Own Warship" - HMS CAMBRIAN had strong Welsh connections throughout her service career but also suffered the ignominy of being broken up in the Welsh Yard of Thomas Ward at Briton Ferry. She arrived on the 6th September 1971 but work didn't start until January the following year. Work was officially declared complete on the 1st September 1972.

(Doug Byrde)

The Weapon Class destroyer HMS CROSSBOW seen arriving at Briton Ferry on the 21st January 1971. It was some two years later on the 15th January 1973 that demolition work commenced. By the 17th August all work was complete and what had been HMS CROSSBOW was no more.

(Doug Byrde)

Shortly after 7 am on the 15th September 1977 what had been many a young officers' training ship - the frigate TENBY is eased up the River Neath to her final berth in the Thomas Ward yard at Briton Ferry.

(D G Thomas)

Photographed from the same point the world's first gas turbine propelled frigate sized warship - HMS EXMOUTH - is hauled the final few yards to the Steel Supply wharf at Skewen on a cold February day in 1979. Towed initially to Swansea docks (by ROYSTERER) on 6th February she was finally taken to the breakers yard on the River Neath on 26th February.

(D G Thomas)

After the haul up the Irish Sea by the Navy's three ocean going salvage tugs (ROBUST, ROYSTERER and ROLLICKER) the hulk of the carrier EAGLE arrived in Loch Ryan on the 18th October 1978 - and promptly ran aground.

(Glasgow Herald)

ARRIVING FOR SCRAP - CAIRNRYAN

As can be seen in this photograph the falling tide left her bow a lot higher out of the water than her stern.

(Glasgow Herald)

When EAGLE's sister ship - ARK ROYAL - arrived some two years later the same mistake was not going to be made again and hi-tech laser equipment is reported to have been installed around the loch so that the huge bulk of the carrier could proceed to the breaking up berth at Cairnryan without further mishap.

(P H McCarlie)

Having been laid up in the Gareloch since 1950 it wasn't until 17th December 1957 that the pride of John Brown's Shipyard back in February 1940 was taken less than a mile to the breaker's yard at Faslane. The DUKE OF YORK had been kept in a maintained state during the six years she spent in the loch. As can be seen from this photograph and the diesel exhaust coming from her aft funnel she still had power through her electrical circuits as she arrived in the breaker's yard.

(D G Thomas)

ARRIVING FOR SCRAP - FASLANE

Five days after leaving Portsmouth on the 4th August 1960 the battleship VANGUARD arrived in Faslane. The tugs BUSTLER and SAMSONIA brought her up the Irish sea with ADVICE, CAPABLE and EARNER assisting. Here the local tugs WARRIOR, THUNDERER, CRUISER, WRESTLER, CAMPAIGNER and FORAGER place her gently alongside.

(W M Lenzie)

All the other ships you've seen in this book had some sort of sea going career but not LEVIATHAN. When structurally almost complete in May 1946 work stopped and she was towed to Portsmouth in July that year. She was to remain there until May 1968. The only useful purpose she provided was as a source of spare parts for the Dutch carrier KAREL DOORMAN when the latter was sold to Argentina. Some 22 years - almost to the day - after work stopped on her she is seen here arriving at Faslane for demolition without having done a decent day's work in her life.

(Fitgerald-Owens Collection)

Anyone who served onboard the guided missile trials ship GIRDLE NESS will doubtless have many memories of warm sunny days in the Mediterranean as she tested the Sea Slug missile system onboard between 1959 and 1961. After a lengthy period acting as a harbour accommodation ship at Rosyth she was eventually towed to Faslane for breaking up. She is seen here arriving on the 11th August 1970.

(D G Thomas Collection)

ARRIVING FOR SCRAP - INVERKEITHING

A giant from a bygone era... Stripped of many upper deck fittings the battleship REVENGE just has enough clearance to make it into the breaker's yard at Inverkeithing in September 1948.

(Thomas Ward)

Another giant from another era - HMS RODNEY - arrives at Rosyth on the 27th March 1948 on her way to Inverkeithing for scrap. Note the wartime camouflage still clearly visible on her ship's side. Six men seem to be pulling her alongside very easily!

(D G Thomas collection)

The Rosyth tugs eventually move the huge hulk of the RODNEY just a few miles down the Forth to the breakers yard at Inverkeithing.

(Thomas Ward)

Of no further use to the Royal - or Russian - Navy the remains of the battleship ROYAL SOVEREIGN arrive in the graveyard for most of Britain's battleships at Inverkeithing. This photograph was taken in March 1950.

(Thomas Ward)

With her paintwork in remarkably good condition the aircraft carrier IMPLACABLE reduced to reserve in 1954 and by November the following year was being eased into Ward's Yard at Inverkeithing.

(Thomas Ward)

Paid off in Devonport in December 1959 it took only a few months for all the fuel and stores to be removed from HMS BIRMINGHAM and for her to be placed on the disposal list. By the 2 September 1960 she had been towed from Devonport - by the tugs TYPHOON and SUPERMAN - with her upper deck paintwork still in excellent condition. It was the high quality steel in her hull that was attractive to the breakers - not her gleaming paintwork.

(Thomas Ward)

"Another one for the chop Bill ...." The aircraft carrier THESEUS arrived at Ward's Inverkeithing Yard on the 2nd June 1962 to take her place on the seemingly endless list of ships to be demolished, there being no future role for them in the post war Royal Navy.

(Morris Allen Collection)

The cruiser MAURITIUS ended her days as flagship of the Commander in Chief, East Indies in 1952 but it wasn't until March 1965 that she was towed to Inverkeithing to meet her fate.

(Morris Allen Collection)

A very bedraggled looking AMETHYST having shot to international stardom as hero of the Yangtse Incident in 1949. She was used at Harwich to play herself in a film of the historic action in the Far East. Seen here shortly after filming she arrived at the Plymouth breakers in January 1957.

(P A Vicary)

With no immediate market for the steel she would provide the salvage vessel RFA PRINCE SALVOR was broken up and her hull used as a storage facility for the ensuing scrap whilst berthed alongside the site of the former Plymouth power station.
(D G Thomas Collection)

The same scrapyard was responsible for the demise of the submarine ANDREW (inboard) and RORQUAL having completed their useful days in the submarine flotilla.

(S Goodman Collection)

One of the first County Class guided missile destroyers to be built was HMS HAMPSHIRE, but she had a short sea going career fromMarch 1963 to paying off in April 1976. By April two years later she had been towed from her lay up berth at Chatham to Briton Ferry. She is seen here a few days after delivery by TYPHOON.

(D G Thomas)

The much acclaimed submarine SERAPH eventually arrived at Briton Ferry (see page 26). The railway trucks that would take her steel away to the local smelters are already awaiting on the jetty.

(A Thompson)

The submarine TALLY-HO arrived at Briton Ferry on the 10th February 1967 just days after being purchased by Thomas Ward.
(D G Thomas)

When the cruiser BERMUDA arrived in Wales for demolition she wouldn't quite fit under the road bridge close to the breakers yard at Briton Ferry. She had to be beached for a couple of days at this berth whilst her top masts were removed and she could be towed the final few yards to the demolition berth.

(D G Thomas)

Safely under the road bridge she is berthed astern of an unknown submarine for work to commence.

(D G Thomas)

This particular berth at Britton Ferry was a regular for the demolition of redundant submarines. Here TEREDO has recently arrived and is abandoned on the mud flats. She just awaits the arrival of the men with the acetylene torches.

(D G Thomas)

After her somewhat difficult tow to the Welsh breakers this view of SERAPH on the Briton Ferry mud gives a good idea of how she had been altered from a conventional S Class submarine with the additional cladding around her hull and streamlined conning tower - all dating back to her days as a target boat.

(A Thompson)

With all her upper works removed the basic hull of URSA lies on the mud at Cashmore's Yard in Newport during May 1968. She had arrived in September the previous year (towed by the tug CYCLONE) but work was not started immediately.

(A Thompson)

Before... Not the most photographed vessel in the fleet but still a vessel worth purchasing as far as a scrap dealer was concerned. Here the boom defence vessel BARRAGE is seen shortly after arriving in the breakers yard at Briton Ferry.

(D G Thomas)

After... After just a few months just about half the demolition work is complete.

(D G Thomas)

One of the group of destroyers that sank the Japanese Cruiser HAGURO and later saw service in the Dartmouth Training Squadron. The Type 15 frigate HMS VENUS was placed in reserve in 1964, however by October 1969 a target ship was needed to test the new Sea Dart guided missile. The VENUS (and WHIRLWIND) were selected for the role. Even here in the breakers yard at Britton Ferry she still carries the markings from her days as a target. Even this work ended in 1972 and she was towed from Pembroke Dock to Briton Ferry for the cutters to get to work.

(D G Thomas)

Not much left. All that remains of the Coastal Minesweeper APPLETON at Briton Ferry on 6th January 1977 is her stern - the rest of the vessel having been taken away. Note the Arabic pennant numbers on her stern. Her last active role had been in the Gulf Squadron.

(D G Thomas)

Waiting for the men with the burning torches to arrive TENBY sits on the mud at Thomas Ward's Yard at Briton Ferry in September 1977.

(D G Thomas)

The final days for the frigate EXMOUTH - seen here in February 1979 on the River Neath. Within a very few months there was not much left to show after the breakers had been at work. Note the single screw which characterised this class of frigate.

(D G Thomas)

Taking the punishment... The frigate GALATEA after worldwide RN service ended her days in a very sorry state. Every conceivable weapon that needed testing seems to have been let loose at her. She eventually slipped beneath the waves on 22 June 1988. No work for the scrapman but plenty of valuable data gained and rare practical experience by missile crews.

(R N Photo)

HMS NUBIAN
(R N Photo)

Sharp eyed readers will notice that we have taken them clockwise around the coast with photographs showing vessels laid up... being towed away ... arriving in the breakers... and then some shots of the breakers starting their work. In our third part of this book we will have some dramatic shots taken actually in the breakers yards - particularly from Inverkeithing - and those taken of sinkings on the high seas too. All thanks to the wealth of material sent in by the readers of *Warship World* magazine.

We would particularly like to thank Dr Ian Buxton and Ben Warlow (the authors of Part 1 of this book) for their help in checking the captions in this edition.

We will of course be advising all those customers who bought this book and its predecessor direct from ourselves when the third edition is available.

INDEX